ANALYZE ADVERSITY.

- ❏ There are four ways to respond to a crisis: *Maximize* it. *Minimize* it. *Advertise* it. *Analyze* it.

- ❏ Maximizing... is to *exaggerate* the crisis. Minimizing... is to *understate* the crisis. Advertising... is to *tell* the whole world about it. Analyzing... is *extracting* useful information from it.

- ❏ Crisis is *merely concentrated information*. Adversity is simply your enemies' reaction to your progress. Taking the time to analyze it will benefit you.

DAY
2

DON'T PANIC.

❑ Something may happen today that shocks you. Don't worry about it. *God anticipated it*.

❑ Remember, satan is merely an ex-employee of Heaven. God knows him quite well. He *fired* him.

❑ Get alone today in the presence of God. Fear will die and courage will flourish.

DAY
3

PURSUE WORTHY COUNSEL.

☐ *Someone knows something you need to know.* Something that can help you survive and even succeed in the most painful chapter of your life.

☐ Ignorance can be deadly. *Don't' risk it.*

☐ Whatever you do today, take the time to *listen* to godly advice. *True champions do.*

WISDOM FROM THE WORD

"Where no counsel is, the people fall: but in the multitude of counsellors there is safety."
Proverbs 11:14

DAY
4

TRUST GOD TO STOP THE ATTACK.

❑ You serve a very capable God. He can turn the hearts of Kings.

❑ You are on His mind this very moment. Your tears, your pain and fears are very important to Him.

❑ He is about to move. *Trust Him*.

WISDOM FROM THE WORD

"He maketh wars to cease"
Psalms 46:9

DAY
5

KEEP THE SPIRIT OF A FINISHER.

☐ Anyone can *begin* a marathon. Champions *finish* them.

☐ Everyone experiences adversity. It is those who stay strong *to the finish* who are rewarded.

☐ *Pace yourself.* Determine to "go the distance." Keep aflame the *Spirit of a Finisher.*

DAY
6

FOCUS ON THE BENEFITS OF ENDURANCE.

❏ Every battle is for a *reason*. Every battle is for a *season*. Don't forget it... ENDURE.

❏ When you are tired, exhausted and discouraged: ENDURE.

❏ Endurance is rewarded. *Always! It is the only thing in eternity that will be rewarded.*

WISDOM FROM THE WORD

"...But he that endureth to the end shall be saved."
Matthew 10:22

DAY
7

DON'T FEEL ALONE TODAY.

☐ You may feel targeted by hell. Your world may be crashing around you. *Don't feel alone.*

☐ Those closest to you may not show it, but *they are hurting, too.*

☐ So, don't yield to self pity. *Pity parties merely postpone your victory.* You are not alone.

WISDOM FROM THE WORD

"Be sober, be vigilant; because your adversary the devil, as a roaring lion, walketh about, seeking whom he may devour: Whom resist steadfast in the faith, knowing that the same afflictions are accomplished in your brethren that are in the world."

I Peter 5:8, 9

DAY
8

SEE THE BIG PICTURE.

❑ *Nothing is ever as it first appears.*

❑ Pain passes. Adversity passes. Look beyond your current hardships. *Something incredible is being produced.*

❑ The resurrection followed the crucifixion. Promotion follows adversity. So get your eyes on the *bigger* picture.

WISDOM FROM THE WORD

"For our light affliction, which is but for a moment, worketh for us a far more exceeding and eternal weight of glory"
II Corinthians 4:17

DAY
9

GUARD YOUR MIND.

❑ Your mind is the *birthplace*... the *incubator*... the *beginning point* of everything you do.

❑ Satan knows this. His entire strategy is to *break* your focus, *sabotage* your concentration and *abort* your assignment from God.

❑ So the *real battleground of life is your mind*. Guard it well.

WISDOM FROM THE WORD

"Finally brethren, whatsoever things are true, whatsoever things are honest, whatsoever things are just, whatsoever things are pure, whatsoever things are lovely, whatsoever things are of good report; if there be any virtue and if there be any praise, think on these things."
Philippians 4:8

DAY
10

REMEMBER, SEASONS CHANGE.

❏ *Attacks don't last forever.*

❏ People change. Weather changes. Circumstances change. So don't be discouraged today. *Expect* supernatural and dramatic changes.

❏ Tomorrow is coming. *Your future is unlike any yesterday you have ever known.*

DAY
11

CREATE YOUR PRAYER CIRCLE.

- ❏ *One cannot multiply.*

- ❏ Increase begins with two. Jesus promised results from the Prayer of Agreement.

- ❏ Make a list of seven effective intercessors for your life. Contact them. They are your *Circle of Protection.*

WISDOM FROM THE WORD

"Again I say unto you, That if two of you shall agree on earth as touching any thing that they shall ask, it shall be done for them of my Father which is in heaven."
"For where two or three are gathered together in my name, there am I in the midst of them."
Matthew 18:19, 20

DAY
12

READ THE STORIES OF CHAMPIONS.

❑ People are different. Some are losers. Some are champions. *Study the champions*.

❑ Meditate on the Biblical accounts of David, Abraham, Joseph, the apostle Paul. Visit your local library. Read the biographies of great men.

❑ Readers become leaders. Read, read, *read*.

WISDOM FROM THE WORD

"Who through faith subdued kingdoms, wrought righteousness, obtained promises, stopped the mouths of lions, Quenched the violence of fire, escaped the edge of the sword, out of weakness were made strong, waxed valiant in fight, turned to flight the armies of the aliens..." Hebrews 11:33, 34

DAY
13

FOCUS ON FASTING.

❑ Adversity is a season of *unusual* attack. So, consider using *unusual weapons*.

❑ Fasting is a *feared weapon* in battle. It is a tool that sharpens your spiritual sensitivity to God.

❑ *Use it.*

WISDOM FROM THE WORD

"Is not this the fast that I have chosen? to loose the bands of wickedness, to undo the heavy burdens, and to let the oppressed go free, and that ye break every yoke?
Isaiah 58:6

DAY
14

REMEMBER THE POWER OF PRAISE.

❑ *Praise is your verbal and physical response to the greatness of God.*

❑ Music... singing... worship... creates an atmosphere for miracles. You are responsible for the climate you permit around you.

❑ *The atmosphere you permit determines the product you produce.*

WISDOM FROM THE WORD

"Let the high praises of God be in their mouth, and a twoedged sword in their hand... to bind their kings with chains... to execute upon them the judgment written: this honour have all his saints. Praise ye the Lord."
Psalms 149:6-9

DAY
15

EXPECT RESCUE.

❑ Adversity is just a page, not your whole book.

❑ *Adversity is simply hell's attempt to abort the next season of blessing God has scheduled for your life.*

❑ The eyes of your Father are upon you. Expect a miraculous rescue.

WISDOM FROM THE WORD

"The Lord upholdeth all that fall, and raiseth up all those that be bowed down."
Psalms 145:14

DAY
16

FIND SOMEONE ELSE IN TROUBLE.

❑ *Your worth is determined by the kinds of problems you are willing to solve for someone.*

❑ Mechanics solve car problems. Lawyers solve legal problems. Doctors solve physical problems.

❑ You are a walking solution to someone in trouble. *Find them.*

WISDOM FROM THE WORD

"And if thou draw out thy soul to the hungry, and satisfy the afflicted soul; then shall thy light rise in obscurity, and thy darkness be as the noon day: And the Lord shall guide thee continually and satisfy thy soul in drought, and make fat thy bones: and thou shalt be like a watered garden, and like a spring of water, whose waters fail not."
Isaiah 58:10, 11

DAY
17

AVOID VICTIM MENTALITY.

- ❑ *Any wounded animal attracts attack.*

- ❑ *Weakness is an invitation to bullies.* So don't talk nor think like a victim of your circumstances.

- ❑ You are more than a conqueror. *Act* like it. *Talk* like it. The love of God is keeping you today.

WISDOM FROM THE WORD

"Who shall separate us from the love of Christ? Shall tribulation, or distress, or persecution, or famine, or nakedness, or peril, or sword?
"Nay, in all these things we are more than conquerors through him that loved us."
Romans 8:35, 37

DAY
18

TRUST GOD.
LOVE PEOPLE.

- ❏ God never commanded you to trust people.

- ❏ God commanded you to *love* people, and *trust Him*.

- ❏ *Know the difference.* Your joy and victory depends on it.

WISDOM FROM THE WORD

"It is better to trust in the Lord than to put confidence in man."
Psalms 118:8

DAY
19

MARK YOUR ENEMY.

❑ When satan launches a strike against you, it is usually through a *person*.

❑ Your enemy is *anyone who attempts to stop the will of God from being fulfilled in your life*.

❑ Identify and avoid anyone who breaks your focus through stirring up strife and division.

WISDOM FROM THE WORD

"Now I beseech you, brethren, mark them which cause divisions and offences contrary to the doctrine which ye have learned; and avoid them."
Romans 16:17

DAY
20

PURIFY YOURSELF BEFORE GOD.

❑ You are the offspring of a Holy God. This explains your insatiable appetite to live a holy and pure life.

❑ Sin happens. *Just don't cover it up.* Bring it to God.

❑ Repentance is the golden hinge that opens the door to the next season of your life.

WISDOM FROM THE WORD

"Behold, the Lord's hand is not shortened, that it cannot save; neither his ear heavy, that it cannot hear: But your iniquities have separated between you and your God, and your sins have hid his face from you, that he will not hear."
Isaiah 59:1, 2

DAY
21

SOAK YOURSELF IN THE SCRIPTURES.

❏ Your mind is like soil. It will grow *any Seed* you sow into it, *good or bad*.

❏ When you sow *words spoken by God* into your mind, you are sowing energy, life, light and hope *into yourself*.

❏ His Word is like a spiritual vaccination that strips satan of his power against your life.

WISDOM FROM THE WORD

"Unless thy law had been my delights, I should then have perished in mine affliction."
Psalms 119:92
"The law of his God is in his heart; none of his steps shall slide."
Psalms 37:31

DAY
22

REMEMBER WHO IS WITH YOU.

- ❏ *Two are better than one.* God said it. Believe it.

- ❏ You are never, never, *never* alone in this world.

- ❏ Invisible, but undeniable, your Creator is standing beside you this very moment, even as you are reading these very words.

WISDOM FROM THE WORD

"...For he hath said, I will never leave thee nor forsake thee. So that we may boldly say, the Lord is my helper, and I will not fear what man shall do unto me."
Hebrews 13:5, 6

DAY
23

KEEP WALKING.

❏ Picture this. You are in your car. You are driving in a heavy hail-storm. You don't stop... but keep driving knowing you will *move out of the storms range*.

❏ Remember Joseph. Remember David. Every day of adversity was simply a *stepping stone toward the throne*.

❏ *Keep walking.*

WISDOM FROM THE WORD

"When thou passest through the waters, I will be with thee; and through the rivers, they shall not overflow thee: when thou walkest through the fire, thou shalt not be burned; neither shall the flame kindle upon thee, for I am the Lord thy God..."
Isaiah 43:2, 3

DAY
24

NEVER, NEVER, NEVER GIVE UP.

❑ Your dreams and goals are worth any fight, any waiting, any price. *Don't give up.*

❑ Your perseverance demoralizes your enemy. Don't give up.

❑ Patience is a weapon. *Don't give up.*

WISDOM FROM THE WORD

"And Jesus said unto him, No man, having put his hand to the plough, and looking back, is fit for the kingdom of God."
Luke 9:62

DAY
25

LOOK FOR DOUBLE-BLESSING.

❑ Read carefully the accounts of Job, Joseph, Daniel and others. Their adversity always birthed a season of Double-Portion Blessings in their lives.

❑ They discovered that *false accusation is often the last stage before supernatural promotion.*

❑ So look for double-blessing. *Miracles are coming towards you... or going past you every day.* Recognize *them.*

WISDOM FROM THE WORD

"And the Lord turned the captivity of Job, when he prayed for his friends; also the Lord gave Job twice as much as he had before"
Job 42:10

DAY
26

BE TOUGH.

❑ *Life is a collection of battles.* Subsequently, it is also a collection of *victories.*

❑ Reach down deep inside yourself today and call forth your greatest strength.

❑ Today is not a day for weakness. *It is time to be tough.*

WISDOM FROM THE WORD

"If thou faint in the day of adversity, thy strength is small."
Proverbs 24:10

"A wise man is strong; yea, a man of knowledge increaseth strength."
Proverbs 24:5

DAY
27

DEPEND ON THE WISDOM OF GOD.

❑ Jesus said you have received two gifts from God: (1) Your mouth and (2) His wisdom.

❑ Unexpected things may happen today. *Don't worry.* The Holy Spirit within you will rise to the occasion and speak through you.

❑ Relax. Someone greater than you is within you. *Depend on Him.*

WISDOM FROM THE WORD

"Settle it therefore in your hearts, not to meditate before what ye shall answer: For I will give you a mouth and wisdom, which all your adversaries shall not be able to gainsay nor resist."
Luke 21:14, 15

DAY
28

REFUSE GRASSHOPPER TALK.

❑ Moses sent 12 men to spy out the land of Canaan.

❑ Ten of the spies came back speaking words of defeat. "We're nothing, We are like grasshoppers next to those huge giants." These ten were *grasshoppers*.

❑ However, the remaining two were giant-killers. Joshua and Caleb refused grasshopper talk. Instead they declared, "We are well able to overcome the giants." God gave them the land.

WISDOM FROM THE WORD

"And they brought up an evil report of the land which they had searched unto the children of Israel, saying... and there we saw the giants... and we were in our own sight as grasshoppers, and so we were in their sight." Numbers 13:32, 33

DAY
29

GIVE GOD TIME.

☐ Jesus invested His first 30 years in preparation for His ministry. Moses spent 80 years becoming a great leader.

☐ Time is your friend. *Don't hurry.*

☐ Remember-*Patience is the weapon that forces deception to reveal itself.*

WISDOM FROM THE WORD

"The Lord is good unto them that wait for him, to the soul that seeketh him. It is good that a man should both hope and quietly wait for the salvation of the Lord."
Lamentations 3:25, 26

DAY
30

AIM YOUR SEED TOWARD DELIVERANCE TODAY.

❑ *Offerings impress God.* They always have. They always will.

❑ David understood this, and *aimed his Seed like an arrow* to get a message to God.

❑ *It worked.* The plague was *stopped.* So when you plant a special Seed-faith offering to the work of God, expect incredible favor.

WISDOM FROM THE WORD

"And David built there an altar unto the Lord, and offered burnt offerings and peace offerings. So the Lord was intreated for the land, and the plague was stayed from Israel."
II Samuel 24:25

DAY
31

DON'T ACCOMMODATE YOUR ENEMY.

❑ Your *real* enemy and adversary is satan. *Always remember this*.

❑ He wants to destroy you. *Don't yield*. Don't negotiate.

❑ It is unnatural to attempt peace with an enemy. You must *conquer* an enemy.

WISDOM FROM THE WORD

"Neither give place to the devil"
Ephesians 4:27

Decision Page

Will You Accept Jesus As Savior Of Your Life Today?

The Bible says, "That if thou shalt confess with thy mouth the Lord Jesus, and shall believe in thine heart that God hath raised Him from the dead, thou shalt be saved. For with the heart man believeth unto righteousness; and with the mouth confession is made unto salvation."(Rom. 10:9-10)

To receive Jesus Christ as Lord and Savior of your life, please pray this prayer from your heart today!

"Dear Jesus, I believe that you died for me and rose again on the third day. I confess I am a sinner. I need Your love and forgiveness. Come into my life, forgive my sins, and give me eternal life. I confess You now as my Lord. Thank You for my salvation, Your peace and joy. Amen."

Return This Today!

❑ Yes, Mike! I made a decision to accept Christ as my personal Savior today. Please send me my free gift copy of your book "31 Keys To A New Beginning" to help me with my new life in Christ. (B48)

"Sow A Seed Of Wisdom Into The Lives Of Those You Love!"

Here is your opportunity to invest in the lives of your Love Circle. Purchase 2 copies of *Seeds of Wisdom On Adversity* for only $5 for 2 special people in your life. These dynamic daily devotionals are your answer to the "Daily Bread" of the Wisdom of God.

❑ Yes, Mike, I want to Sow 2 *Seeds of Wisdom On Adversity* into 2 people that I love. I have enclosed $5 for the 2 books. Please rush them immediately. (SOW098)

B21

Send A Self-Addressed Envelope With Check Or Money Order To: Mike Murdock
P.O. Box 99 • Dallas, TX • 75221

Wisdom Book Libraries

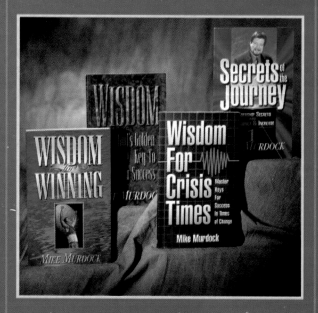

The Winner's Book Library

Wisdom Book Libraries

The Assignment Book Library

All 4 Books
For Only
$20⁰⁰

1. The Assignment/Volume 1:
   (The Dream & The Destiny)
   (167 pages)—$10⁰⁰

2. The Assignment/Volume 2: (The Anointing &
   The Adversity) (204 pages)—$10⁰⁰

3. 31 Facts About Wisdom (48 pages)—$7⁰⁰

4. Secrets Of The Journey/Volume 2 (32 pages)—$5⁰⁰

Wisdom Book Libraries

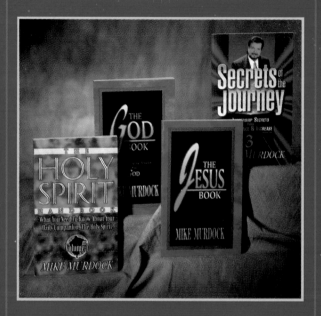

The Holy Spirit Book Library

1. The Holy Spirit Handbook (166 pages)—$10⁰⁰

2. The God Book (167 pages)—$10⁰⁰

3. The Jesus Book (173 pages)—$10⁰⁰

4. Secrets Of The Journey/Volume 3 (32 pages)—$5⁰⁰

Wisdom Book Libraries

The Leadership Book Library

All 4 Books For Only $20⁰⁰

1. The Leadership Secrets of Jesus (196 pages)—$10⁰⁰

2. 3 Most Important Things In Your Life (256 pages)—$10⁰⁰

3. 31 Secrets for Winning at Work (112 pages)—$14⁰⁰

4. Secrets Of The Journey/Volume 4 (32 pages)—$5⁰⁰

Wisdom Book Libraries

The Millionaire's Book Library

1. Secrets of the Richest Man Who Ever Lived (178 pages)—10^{00}

2. 31 Reasons People Do Not Receive Their Financial Harvest (256 pages)—12^{00}

3. 31 Secrets to Career Success (112 pages)—10^{00}

4. Secrets Of The Journey/Volume 5 (32 pages)—5^{00}

Wisdom Book Libraries

Wisdom For Women Book Library

1. The Proverbs 31 Woman
   (80 pages)—$7⁰⁰

2. 31 Secrets of an Unforgettable Woman
   (181 pages)—$9⁰⁰

3. Dear Misty (70 pages)—$7⁰⁰

4. Secrets Of The Journey/Volume 6
   (32 pages)—$5⁰⁰

Wisdom Book Libraries

The Dreamer's Book Library

1. Dream Seeds
   (104 pages)—$9^{00}

2. 7 Keys to 1000 Times More (124 pages)—$10^{00}

3. The Covenant of 58 Blessings (87 pages)—$8^{00}

4. Secrets Of The Journey/Volume 7
   (32 pages)—$5^{00}

Item	Title	Qty.	Price	Total
WBL-1	The Winner's Book Library		$20	$
WBL-2	The Assignment Book Library		$20	$
WBL-3	The Holy Spirit Book Library		$20	$
WBL-4	The Leadership Book Library		$20	$
WBL-5	The Millionaire's Book Library		$20	$
WBL-6	The Wisdom for Women Book Library		$20	$
WBL-7	The Dreamer's Book Library		$20	$
Canada Add 20% for Currency Difference				$
U.S. Add 10% Shipping				$
Canada Add 20% Shipping				$
Enclosed is My Seed-Faith Gift for Your Ministry				$
Total				**$**

MasterCard • VISA • AMEX • DISCOVER
Sorry, No COD's

Name

Address

City

State

Province

Country

Zip   Telephone

Method of Payment:

❏ Check ❏ Money Order
❏ Visa ❏ MasterCard ❏ AMEX ❏ Discover

Signature_____

Exp. Date _____

Card No.

Clip & Mail This Form To:
Mike Murdock Ministry
P.O. Box 99 • Dallas, Texas • USA • 75221
940-464-3020 • FAX 940-464-4012